CHANGING TIDES

ABOUT THE AUTHOR

Vicky Foster has lived all her life in a city
where the rivers can still stop the traffic,
where waters can overrun the streets and
where festivals and nights out are held on
piers and marinas. Living there, she has
developed a great love for her city, but
also the realisation that there are some
things you can never control and that

often the best thing to do is learn to ride the tides. Like the
water, poetry has always been there for Vicky – but at the
age of 18 she decided to put down her pen and go and find
something to write about. In her unique poetic voice, Vicky
shares with us vivid images of the many changes which life
has washed up, in the years between then and now. This
book, in the *Humber Sound* series, *Changing Tides*, is her first
published collection of poems.

CHANGING TIDES

POEMS BY

VICKY FOSTER

THE STARING OWL

2016

ISBN 978-1-909548-66-4
CHANGING TIDES
is typeset in
Book Antiqua and Gill Sans
and published by
The King's England Press
111 Meltham Road
Lockwood
HUDDERSFIELD
West Riding of Yorkshire

© Vicky Foster 2016
2nd impression 2019

The Staring Owl is the poetry imprint
of The King's England Press

Printed and bound in the UK
by Lulu Press
digital print on demand

I dedicate this book to my two beautiful boys,
who were made in Hull, from girders.

HIGH TIDE

There will be days when we
Are full.
When we are buoyant.
When a fresh sea breeze clears
Everything away
And sunlight
Glints on the water,
And anything seems possible.

THE COLOURED BIRD

The Coloured bird
Is back today.

Rolling vivid polaroids
And posting them
Into my ears.

They unfurl lazily
Inside my head,
Stretching long corners
Into my brain.

And I hear her voice then.

Singing
In every colour.

Painting crotchets
And semi-quavers

Into landscapes
Of ochre, magenta,
Cerulean and jade.

Her voice
Like brushstrokes
Along the soft inner curve
Of my skull.

STARTING SOMEWHERE

My tiny sandal
Once nestled
In the hollow
Of a giant footstep.

My long white socks
Amid an ocean
Of freshly crushed
Brown earth.

When I opened my mouth,
No sound loud enough
To penetrate
The giant roars and bellows,
Could find its way out.

And though my eyes
Searched endlessly,
The horizon
Was always obscured.
By a forest
Of giant tree-trunk legs.

And I lived
With this view,
This quiet acceptance,
Having known no other way.

Until one day
I realised
That even giants
Must have started out
Tiny.

And so I decided
To grow.

SECRET CODES

As pebbles marked with letters
Drop into the pool of your mind,
You laugh and smile.
Holding them
Like you will
The rest of your life.

A new language.
A secret code.

And we spell out words
Like mum.
Like love.
Like you
And me.
Like us.

And I decide that this
Is the language
You will learn
And grow with.

Simple as wooden blocks
Stacked
One on top of another.

So that we can climb
And climb
Until far below
The people are cartoon figures

And when they shout
It only sounds cheerful.

All gestures mollified
By distance.

ABOUT THAT SUMMER

That summer,
The sun and the rain
Poured from the sky
In equal measure.

And gardens grew wild
With herbs and spinach.

I hoarded and boiled it.

I pushed it into tiny square cubes
And froze it.

Storing up strength
For the months that were coming.

And long after the sun went in,
I fed you
On the hope
That was planted
All those months earlier,

Before winds tore up roots
And frost killed delicate
Leaves and stems.

ROOTS

I had a tree once.

You knew it was mine
Because my initials were on it.

And Sarah's
And Lois's
And Danielle's.

Fingerprints
From all the boys we kissed
Marked the branches.

And fag ends
That tasted
Of fried egg sandwiches
And coffee with two sugars
And UHT milk,
Staked out the boundary around it.

They were dusted with cinnamon
From the time we tried to smoke it,
And broken bits of eye shadow
And cheap face powder
We bought in Boyes's.

If I pick up the fir cones
And listen,
I hear echoes of our talks.

And the leaves reflect
Pictures of us
Fighting
In the trees,

Laughing
On the way to school,

Laying in the sun
Writing poems.

Hiding under Giant's Table
When the rain came.

Before we all moved on.

SMIGGY

We tumbled through those days
Like carefree stigs,
With a Toblerone up each sleeve
And a pocketful of 20p singles.

Cadging change, sniffing gas,
Hopping rowing boats to islands.
Chasing Pedal & Pop as far as we could
Before his engine finally kicked in.

Stolen booze
On the school field.
Stolen moments
On the school roof.

I jangled with silver charms
And you, long-legged,
Smiling and awkward,
Made music out of jibes.

Bouncing bushes, getting a chase,
We gathered in alleys and
Empty living rooms.

Our eyes spoke languages
Others couldn't understand,
Made plans that flew and danced
And got carried away on the breeze
Like dandelion clocks.

Make a wish.
Make a wish, quick,
Before it blows away.

And I wish for East Park
In the sunshine.

For winning at Block.

For finding you
After too long looking,
Crouched on the rocks
By the animal cages

Like you'd been there
All along.

THE DAY I NEARLY DIED

The day I nearly died
Didn't happen.
Though some people
May tell you it did.

Somehow my valves
Were set to run
Like a leaky tap.

And while blood ebbed
In a long flow
Of hours,

I remained.

A pause
In a flesh and blood
Restroom.
A bookmark
In a day,
Before the rest
Of my life began.

With the weight
Of two softly sleeping
Children

Holding me firm here.

A DROP IN THE OCEAN

There was a time
When a kind word
From you

Would have fallen
Like rain
On scorched earth.

When I would have
Soaked it up.

It could have
Nourished me.

But you couldn't
Spare a drop.

And I grew anyway,
Stunted.

And eventually,
After long hot years,

People came
Who poured
Their kindness
Over and through me.

I swam in deep pools.
I eased away all nightmares
Of famine and drought.

And now you come,
With too late

Too small drops
To give to me.

And I barely hear
The tiny splash

As they land,
Inconsequential,
Along my cool,
Luxurious
Surface.

THE MOTHS

There are moths
Living under
My ribcage.
Sometimes
I forget
They're there -
But then
There's the mad
Fluttering
Of wings
To remind me.

They feast
On not-forgotten things.
Things I've put away.
Things I've packed up.
Things I wish
I had forgotten.

But I haven't.
And neither
Have the moths.

So one day soon
I'll start to look.
I'll face the fusty mess,
Festering and faded.

I'll open up those boxes.

Show them to the sun.

And let the moths
Fly up
In my face,

Before I say
Goodbye.

THE CALL

I lost my heart
On the Wolds one day
Circa 1989.

I paused
To breathe in the view
And as it filled and hovered
It hooked on greening
Springtime branches.

And now it hangs, half empty,
Waiting for the wind
To resonate

At just my frequency
So that it calls to me,
And I race back there
To fill my eyes
With rolling fields,
Lay fingers on bark.
Place feet on earth.

Stretching cells
Out and across
Until they sing back

We found it.
We found it -

And for a while
I'm like a finished jigsaw,

All my pieces slotting
Satisfyingly into place.

A HIGH TIDE AT LAST

I give you to the river.
I give you up.
I watch you go.
Buffeted by waves,
Brown water washes you.

I watch you go.
And I'm OK.

And I know that
When the water ebbs

You won't be there,
Waiting in the mud.

This time
You are gone.

Carried away
On a swift high tide
To the next port
And beyond.

To rest somewhere new.

Because this time
I let you go.

I do not rope you
And risk us both
Being dragged
And pulled
And swallowed
In heavy sucking mud.

This time,
I let you go.

GIVING UP

She stands.
One foot on cracked old tiles
And the other cushioned
By crisp winter blackness.

Eyes on the stars
As smoke curls from her lips
And one hand curves
Protectively
Over a still-flat tummy.

"This will be my last one –
For now at least."
And eyes glance briefly down
At the cigarette
Carelessly cradled
Between two fingers.

The warm taste of whisky
Still lingers on lips
That search
To find the words
For everything she can see and feel
Spread out in the night sky before her.

For all the old pleasures and comforts.
For ease, for one-ness
And a head that can lie
On a pillow at night
And rest easy.
For soft smooth skin
And admiring glances.
To be taut and firm
And fresh and free.

To be ripe and young and creative.

To know what all of that is –
And to step away anyway,
Knowing.

She lingers,
Last glowing breaths
Of cigarette
Warming the tips of her fingers,
While the tang of tobacco
In cold night air
Fills her lungs.

Half in, half out -
She turns to call to him.
Her eyes search his
For understanding,
For empathy,
For some acknowledgement
Of all she can see now,
Spread out before her.

Not finding that,
She recognises
A new truth
Instead.

Some love
That seems to burn so bright,
Can be puffed out
In a breath of smoke.

THE ALCHEMIST

What if
Every sorrow you ever
Bled for
Turned out to be
The strength in
Your marrow?

What if
Everything you ever
Felt bound by
Turned out to be
The girdle
Holding you straight?

What if
Worry and wonder and
Restless hours
Were the cement
In your layers?

What if
You were the Alchemist
All along?

And every thought,
Every brick,
Every ordinary moment
Laying action upon idea,
Smoothing lines
And easing out bubbles
Turned out to be

The daily grind
Of an artist

At work?

What if
You were the Alchemist
All along?

Transforming
Hard and cold
And gritty and brittle

Into
Glowing warmth
Gleaming and strong?

What if
The boring sameness
Of grey and black
Tarmac
Didn't matter?

But what mattered most
Was how you laid it,
And where it led
When you finished?

Maybe people never stop
And praise the way
You get the mix just right,

Balancing sand and cement
And water.

And what if it still doesn't matter?

Because when your figure -
Stretching, bending, lifting, laying -

Is no longer a distraction,

And all the action
In the foreground is stilled,

And people look up
And see what you were building
All this time,

It just might take their breath away.

LOW TIDE

And sometimes we will empty.
Sometimes there will only be
Thick, black mud
As far as the eye can see.

And we will be stuck here,
For a while, at least.

WHAT WE SAY INSTEAD

It's easy to say
It's probably
For the best.

Those words lie over
Everything else
We could think instead.

Like a screen
Blocking out
The running film
Of happy possibilities.

The sad facts
Standing like
Layered muslin

So that we can't see
Each one
On its own.

And the muted
Colours behind
Flowing in
Indistinguishable shapes,

So that we
Have to focus
Our attention
Elsewhere.

COMING OVER

I dreamed again
About the bridge.

About the way it creaks
And lifts

Just as my bus reaches
It's apex.

I bang on the windows.

I shout for the driver.

Other people
Carry on talking.

Like they can't see
Anything wrong.

But I know
What's coming.

I feel us
Beginning to tip
And fall.

I'm waiting
For the deep splash
And the heavy

Slap

As cold water closes
Over our heads

And we are lost.

Again.

PITFALLS

As a very small child
I started falling down holes.

People didn't notice at first.

The whiff of a shadow
Against their shoulder
Or a slight shiver
Might make them turn,

But I was up on my feet again
Before they could complete
A revolution.

Things could disappear
Like dust back then.

And holes in air are soon covered
With words
Or filled
With new actions.

And it went on
This way.

Until I moved to a place
Where the climate was better
And less prone
To invisible seismic
Shifting.

And bit by bit
I grew more confident
Of my feet on solid ground.

I walked with purpose
And stopped second guessing
Whether the air in front of my eyes
Was about to open up
And swallow me.

But with time,
I came to realise

That those holes
Had never disappeared
At all.

They had fragmented,
And fallen in through my pores
Like ground glass.

So that every time
I was ready
To shed a layer of skin

I had to look in
At a million tiny fragmented
Mirrors

And find out
What they were made of.

AFTERNOON DRIVES

The after-school
Friday afternoon
Drive
Was the worst
Part of the week.

The sick tummy.
The too-warm
Can't wind the window down
Cos people will be
Angry. Stop being selfish
Bitch
Drive. Was the worst
Bit.

Too much in a
Small space.

Cars aren't big enough
For all that.

And neither are
Eight-year old

Girls.

NEARLY PERFECT

He measured my body
Against the picture
In his head
And told me
I was nearly perfect.

It would be twenty years
Before I realised
How wrong he was.

And so the words
Crawled down
Into my stomach
And stayed.

Bigger words,
Sliding on scaly bellies
And forking hissing tongues

Soon swallowed them.

And they grew
And they bred
And before I knew it

My gut was writhing and teeming
In a bloated painful mass.

And even so,
From time to time,

I would open my mouth
And let some new monster
Snake its way down my throat
To join them.

FAIRYTALES

PART 1: THE PRINCESS & THE BATH WATER

You found me in ashes.
Coated in a film of soot.

I'd thought to stay

But you thought different.
You told me

That I was a princess.

And my face laughed
To think of it.

But quietly
My heart whispered

Yes.

Yes please.

And so
I rode with you.

White horses
And long dresses.

And with soft words
And warm water

You showed me
What you saw
Beneath the debris

I carried.

And then you drank
The bath water.

PART 2: KNIGHTS & DRAGONS

Beneath your
Shining armour
I'd thought to find
Soft skin and belly.

But you were encrusted
With muddy layers
Like some dull dragon
Who knew
It should have had
Emeralds and rubies
Instead.

And I know you felt
A yearning
To get clean.

How I would
Have loved
To soak away
Hardened hurts.

But you wore your scales
Like another armour.

The strange calcified growths
Were weapons.

And in the end
I had to put up walls

To keep you out.

PART 3: LET DOWN YOUR HAIR

You called
From beyond
My armaments,
And knowing your disguise,
I pretended
Not to hear

At first.

But your words
Held magic,
And you always knew
How to use them
Against me,

And so they twined,
Vinelike,
Finding crevices
Along my walls,
Around my ears,
Between
My fingers.
Before settling
And filling
Aching voids.

Pressing tenderly
Against still soft

Centres.

And I let down
My hair.

THE ONE THAT GOT AWAY

You bend words
Like Uri Geller
And wriggle free
Like Houdini.

You twist and turn
Like the fish
That just missed
The hook.

And I am powerless –
Line running
Through my fingers
Too fast
For me to catch it.

I'm missing my chance.
I know I am.
I thought I had you
This time.

Thought I could
Scoop you up
And show you around.

Look. Look at him
Now.
See him
When the sun shines

On his scales.

See who he is
Now.

But the line runs
Through my fingers
And you slide
Back into the
Cool blue water.

Smiling an oily
Smile.

Just for me.

OK

There's someone on the phone.
A man's been arrested.
But it's not what they say.
It's OK.

There's a knock at the door.
Policemen on the couch.
They just want to talk.
It's OK.

There's detectives on the couch.
There's a story on the news.
There's a body in a skip.
A man's been arrested.

They just want to talk.
They just want to know.

Right from the start.

And it's not OK
It's not OK.

MEN IN UNIFORM

A man in uniform
Knows things.

A man in uniform
Knows things
Better than you.

A woman
With a clipboard
Knows things.

She knows things
Better than you.

And doctors
In clean white coats
With their bright
White lights -

And judges.
And solicitors.

They all know better than you.

And the weight of all they know -

Of their powerful paraphernalia -

Is heavy enough to crush you.

And it does crush you.

And then you are dust

Waving on the breeze

Their breath makes.

Blowing wherever their words send you.

So let's hope they're watching

What they say.

NIGHT TERRORS

You cried
That night.
And many
That went before.

You'd dreamed again.
Your Daddy –
In a big castle.

With bars
On the windows.

He was crying.
He was scared.

And I knew

I had to take you there.

I thought
It couldn't be worse
Than what you dreamed.

And it seemed to help.

But afterwards -
I couldn't sleep.

It was the sight
Of the man
With monsters
Under his bed.

With iron bars
Across his mouth.

He was crying.
He was scared.

And I knew
There was nothing
Anyone could do

To make him better.

LET'S START DIGGING

And the woman
Behind the counter said

Go and ask your Daddy

And he said

That's not my Daddy

My Daddy
Is in
Prison

And I just wanted
The ground
To swallow
Me
Up.....

I

Look

At you

At your whiningselfabsorbed
Howveryembarrassing
Thatthisshouldhappentome

Smug face.
Tight like a mouth
About to spit.

And I realise that

I want the ground
To swallow you up
Too.

It's time for you to go.

SHADOW MAN

I hide their eyes.
I block their view.
Passing noticeboards
And paper stands
That tell the end of you.

The Shadow Man.
Sending out flares.
Even now
They hang in a sky
That no longer
Shapes to your presence.

But physical things
No longer bending
For you,
There still buzzes
Your echo
Around me.

In corners,
In dark rooms,
Your presence
Taps out
On spider legs.

And sometimes shows itself.

Reflections in windows
And strangers' faces.

It should feel safe
To scream back now.
But relief is not entire.

Because of the shadows.

And sleep brings dreams of
Ink blots soaking in pages,
Blood seeping into concrete,

And the realisation that
Some stains
Can never
Be scrubbed

Clean.

WHAT YOU THOUGHT

You thought you felt
The scratch of dirt
Along the walls
Of your veins
And arteries.

But I could have told you
That something shimmered there.

You thought the dust
On your pores and eyelids
Was attracted like to likeness.

But I could have shown you
Bright skin and iris.

You thought that lips
Embellished with lies
Were the only ones
For kissing.

But I could have given you
Nakedness meeting.

And so when blood and skin
And eye and mouth
Were pummeled
And cracked open,
And all your beautiful faces
Spilled out
In the night
To lie in the gutter
Before evaporating,

I could have whispered -

See, they were there all along.

KEEP BRITAIN TIDY – PART I

My life is not a tidy place to live.

Stuff spills out of drawers
And cupboards to litter
My clean floors
And carpets.

Cobwebs swirl the lights
In vivid grey and darkening black
And throw their hue
On everything.

Cracked glass panes
Distort the light.

And muddied,
It fails to bring me clarity.

So I roam the rooms.
I clean the toilets
And the sinks.

I wash my hands.
I wash my hands.

But all the sea
Cannot wash away
The darkness
In my house.

My life is not a tidy place to live.

KEEP BRITAIN TIDY – PART 2

My head is not a tidy place to live.

Broken bits of memories fall
To scatter and litter
My clean life.
My goodness.

They leave behind
Emotions like bad smells.
Spoiling days and
Casting shadows.

And I rummage.
And I rummage.

Scraping knuckles
In the fragments.

On the sharp bright shards.

I shout for you.
I shout for you.

But no-one else
Can find me here.

My arms are weak
And cannot scrub.

My head is not a tidy place to live.

KEEP BRITAIN TIDY – PART 3

I open my mouth
To shout for you

But I don't know you.
I don't know you yet.

I open my mouth
To shout anyway

But heavy black bugs
Fall out.

They run around me,
Mocking me.

They scrabble
Over arms and legs
To nip and bite at me.

Next time
I don't open my mouth
At all.

But too long passes.

I open my mouth
To shout again.

There are no sounds.
I feel breath
Rushing over my lips,
Cool and light.

It's too light.
These are not words.

They are thin
Grey smoke.

It washes uselessly
Over smug sharp faces.

It fills my eyes
And nose and mouth.
I cannot breathe

My legs don't work
My arms don't work -
Even my body betrays me now.

My life is not a tidy place to live.

DEMOLITION DAY

We said we'd gather
And watch

As they blew a part
Of our landscape
To tiny bits of dust
And rubble.

A barbecue.
A celebration.

Probably
A good defence.
Remember what's still here

While something
So huge,
So sturdy,
Tall and strong -

Suddenly crumbles to nothing.

It was a good plan.
I liked it.

And I tried and tried
To get there.

But my boys and me,
We were stuck in a car
On the other side of town.

Wheels spinning in air.
Windows blinded
By thick dust.

I tried to call

But you were all
Too far away.

And you couldn't
Hear us

For the blast.

BATTLE LINES

He sits.

Pages spread before him
On the table

And floating around his head.

Flapping in breezes
Blown in on Viking rivers

On the movement of air
Pushed up by the
Marching feet of Romans

And conquistadors.

Eyes far away
Seeing the intricacies
Of a thousand battles
And treacherous journeys

But never looking in.

ON ROAD

In this place
People wear words
On their faces
Like scars.

Words like hard,
Cold, and sorry.

Etched under eyes
Like grim tattoos
And scratched into
Foreheads and cheekbones.

Thick black lines
Forming question marks
And exclamation points.

Every muscle in these faces
Has flexed and shifted
Around queried concepts

Too abstract
And intricate
For tongue and cheek alone
To articulate.

And so they walk here.
Stepping in well worn grooves
And sturdy ruts,
Without answers.

Brandishing quiet mouths
And faces that shout
As you pass them.

SPRING TIDE

Spring tide: 1. either of the two tides that occur at or just after new moon and full moon when the tide-generating force of the sun acts in the same direction as that of the moon, reinforcing it and causing the greatest rise and fall in tidal level. The highest spring tides (equinoctial springs) occur at the equinoxes. Compare neap tide
2. any great rush or flood

GOLDEN DAYS

There are dates that have been scratched
Across the surface of my brain.

Little rivulets of golden memories
Have run in and filled them.

So that now they're precious
And painful
All at once.

Some of these dates
Are spent
In snowy graveyards,
With pictures
Of candlelit tables,
Cakes and fairy lights

Hovering
Around my head.

They're hooked
Like bunting
To those golden dates.

And when they play
In the breeze,
The colours glint and shine.

But they pull
In tender places
That might

Never

Heal.

THOSE STORIES

I've been telling myself
Those stories again.
The ones with the shoulds
Like iron bars

That penetrate the ground
And throw up
A humming cloud
Of black bugs.

They undulate
Above my head
And then fly out
To find all my possible paths.

And lay as blockades
Over them.

I shout for you.

I tell you
And you laugh.

And in that moment
I remember who I am again.

The night in the bar
And all those months after.

I look around
And see where I really am.

And we set off
Together
To dance
The *Cucaracha*.

SORRY / NOT SORRY

I'm sorry that I'm a woman
With complex views on subjects
That you can't be arsed
To understand.

I'm sorry that my physical form,
My energy and ideas
Don't fit into the wooden box
You had made for me.

I'm sorry that I can't just live
In this one room you prepared.
But there's the whole house
I want to explore.

And fuck it –

There's the world.

RECIPE FOR DISASTER

This anger wasn't for you.
I made it while you were out.
I sourced the ingredients (same as always).
I prepped them carefully (I'm well practiced).
I started it off on a low heat
And left to simmer until done.

I don't know why I made it,
But you didn't ask for it.

All the same I take it up
And offer it around

When you get home.

Like it's something
I need us all
To have a little
Taste of.

I can't stomach it all.

You snatch up a couple
Of bite-sized appetizers.

Sour,
But you can handle them.

The main course, however,
Is too much.

You throw it back.
Away.
At the walls.

Afterwards,
I watch it drip off the ceiling
And wonder –

1. Why I made it at all?

And

2. What I can make for dessert?

POT LUCK

Aggression
Sits by the salt
On the table
In a cracked clay pot.

A family heirloom.

We put it away
Carefully
Every night,
But like a scene
In some second rate
Horror movie,
It's back again,
Centre place,
When we get up.

And so we dance
Around it.
Pretend
We don't see.

And it fills itself
And fills itself
And fills itself
Until, at last,
It spills.

And we breathe it in ...

And then we're off -
Neural pathways firing
Like a sprint over hot coals.
Like a shot from a gun.

A flare going up.

And afterwards,
Breathless
And choking on the
Mess,

We have to look up
And see
What we've done.

OPEN ME UP

Open me up.
There are cogs and springs
That grind and whir
Out of tune.

You can't see or hear
Anything
Beyond them.

They're playing
A discordant note
That distracts you

And it's all I hear
Too, for now.

But when I close my eyes
I see behind the mess,

A perfect solitary string.

And though I don't hear it yet
I know that

There will come a day
When it will play

A perfect note.

ROCK SOLID

When people ask
Are you ok?
And you say
Yes -
But really
Your heart is breaking
Over things that happened
Ten, twelve, thirty years ago....

That sadness and pain
Are bubbling up
From the place you
Crushed them into
All that time ago?

That pressure and a will
Like rock
Buried those things
Like a dark pool of water
Deep in a solid mountain.

But now that the landscape
Is relaxing,
That pool is forming fissures.
Easing into cracks
And softened arches
And springing forth.
Tears like release

Are melting into
Hardened soil
And finding forgotten seeds.

And you're hoping that
All of it
Might be somehow
Worth it.
If you can only
Find a way

To create
The right conditions
For those seeds

To finally
Grow
And bloom.

ALL THAT GLITTERS

My wedding band holds heavy.
Third finger, left hand.
Metallic maker of memories,
I often stop and weigh it
In my mind and in my palm.
The one tells me of its lightness,
But the other tells me truer.

It's ripened fullness
Waiting to spring.
This ring.

It knows the days I will wear it.
Will unfold goggling eyes on my fate.

It's hiding all its secrets
Inside
Where I can't see them yet.

The nagging gnawing in my gut.
The lightness in my step.
The carefree smile and laden brow -
They're all inside.

And only it knows when and where and how.

And I'm waiting –
Like a kid with a Jack in the Box.

Ready, wound, waiting to see.

What it's gonna loose on me.

Now that I've unfolded tissue thin layers of protection.

Now that I've thrown away the box.
Now that I've taken it into my mind and heart,
Weaving trust with every mechanical turn
Of the handle that drove us here.

I'm waiting.

I close my eyes to make a wish

That, please -
Just this once –

All that glitters can be gold.

HURT

She carries hurt
Neatly.
In small packages.

Like a cabinet
Of curiosities.

Stretching creaking fingers
She peels back flesh
Hard as mahogany
To choose from
Ivory shelving.

Today she'll take a look at this one.

Hands like doilies layered in dust
Can't connect with what's inside.
But she holds them by the paper
All the same.

They glow in new colours.
Distilled and strong.
And she watches the figures
Dancing. Like they're people
She never knew.

She wouldn't like to touch –
She'd break the seals.
And who knows
What they might release?

Fizzing, popping and melting
Into a watercolour mess
Of emotions
And words
And pain....

And the thought of that
Impending peopled tidal wave

Prompts her.
And she quickly puts it back.

Shelves straight.
Flesh locked.

The keeper of the key.

DRAGONFLY

She
Has grown.
Strong, beautiful and agile.

Her skin
Glints in sunshine
Like multi-faceted
Gossamer wings.

She sees her sisters
From a distance.

And she knows,
From way over here,
That they are nimble
And sure.

That they move
With freedom and purpose.

She feels a longing.

And a rising certainty
That she can join them.

She knows what she needs to do,

And she poises herself
Ready to move,
Arms cocked
And impetus loaded.

But every time
She tries to push off

Her flesh
Becomes heavy,

Trapping and pulling at her.

Blank boring eyes

Seem to pin her,

And an insidious voice

Tells her she can't fly.
Tells her she must stay
Weighted against the ground.

And she
Is weighted.

By these words.

And again,
She doesn't fly today.

CROP CIRCLES

We run to the fields in fury
And gaze at the mess.
Ruins. Tatters.
Patterns and shapes
Spread before us
Like a crazy jigsaw.

There's confusion and anger.
How did they get here?

Why? Why? Why?

And as the first of the
Morning sun
Burns away dew
Like the last excuses

We gaze out at the sky
For an answer.

While your lawnmower
Cools in the garage
And we pretend
Not to notice.

SURVIVORS

You can smother me.
Bury me.
Pile your sins upon me
Like rocks.
But this light in my eyes
Will burn.

You can hit me,
Hate me,
Threaten me and
Burn me.
But still my beating heart
Will yearn.

My limbs may ache.
My muscles weak.
My lips may lose the strength
To speak -

But at my ebb
And at my peak,
My blood will pulse
And with each beat

My strength will grow.
Before you know

I fly before you once again
So far
So bright
You cannot see.

Long after you
Remember me,
I will set your memory free.

So I can rise.

CHANGE IS GONNA COME

Change is gonna come.
Unfettered, freed, released
Through burnished branches,
Golden light & falling autumn leaves.

Change is gonna come.
It's the rumble of the earth.
It's the warming of your blood -
It's life and death and birth.

Change is gonna come.
It's racing down the tracks,
It's bearing down upon us.
It's never going back.

Change is gonna come
Blowing up around your face,
Movement, pace, transfigured time.
You'd better take your place.

Change is gonna come
As certain as the spring
When thawing ice breaks
Make your plans - what will you usher in?

Change is gonna come
And then you'll have your peace
As filtered sun traps time stood still.
Some rest, respite, release.

SPREAD YOUR WINGS

Stretch out those new found feathers,
Hold your head up high.
Stop the tremble in your wing tips,
Gaze out across the sky.

Hold steady in your legs.
Make your breathing deep.
Clear your mind and steal your heart,
Prepare to make the leap.

Let the world unfurl before you
As you fly through golden skies.
Let your song spill out to rest among
The stars and butterflies.

Tear fire from the raindrops
To dance in molten rain.
Burn away to start again.
Find glory from your pain.

FINAL WORDS

The day you were born
And the day you died
Are only one month apart.
But they used to be separated
By 31 years.

Now I'm 5 years older
Than you ever were.
But you used
To be 5 older than me.

You were different
To anything I'd ever known,
Broken and beautiful
In a way that cut
Straight through to my gut.

From the start
You felt like someone
Whose feet rested
On the edge
Of a very high drop.

It could all have ended
In blood and dirt
At any moment.

I had no choice
But to hold on to you.
To try and balance out
The gravitational pull
Of that long fall.

But in the end
I just couldn't hold you
Tight enough.

The temptation
To keep edging away,
To keep testing the strength
Of that flimsy ledge
Was always too strong for you.

And now that you've gone
And I've healed some of the hurt
You left behind,

There's something I need to say.

And today seems like the day
To get it said.

The drive is punctuated
By places.

Our first home together.

The house you grew up in.

The roads of late night drives
To soothe a crying baby.

Our final home.

The funeral home
I never visited.
The church we never married in.

The graveyard.

I don't bring things
To leave behind.
I hate to think of them
After I've gone,

Alone in the wind and rain.
Battered to a soggy mess.

And all there was
To be given and taken
Between us
Is done now.

Physical things
Don't matter anymore.

Afterwards
I sit in the shelter
Of a well kept hut,
Looking over the distance
Between us
To where you rest now.

And across the cut grass
These two places are linked

By a set of footprints
In the snow.

The path I walked
To say I'm sorry.

WAKING UP

This morning when I woke,
There beside me on the bed
Was the skin of the woman
I used to be.

I marveled.
Firstly, that I had somehow crawled out
In my sleep.
But mostly, at the shape of it.

How it's contours and wrinkles
Didn't fit the shape I was now.
I wondered how I'd lived
In that shell
For so long.

And then, once the confusion
And the wonder of that old shell
Wore off,

I realised that I felt different.
Lighter somehow.

Comfier.

I realised I needed to look
In the mirror.

I cracked the blinds
To let in the morning light
And as it fell across the room,

Across the mirror,

I felt it.

That fear and excitement
That comes with new pages.

The press of air too heavy
On new skin,

Hard earned
Or much loved things
Almost too special to wear.

And I remembered the long night
Before sleep came.

The splitting and tearing
And cracking open.

And I realised

That maybe
I'd won the right

To these new
And terrifying
Wings.

NEAP TIDE

neap tide (n): (Physical Geography) either of the two tides that occur at the first or last quarter of the moon when the tide-generating forces of the sun and moon oppose each other and produce the smallest rise and fall in tidal level. Compare spring tide.

NEAP TIDES FOREVER NOW

Neap tides forever now.

I've found the moon
That holds me steady.

That hovers
At the perfect distance
Letting me settle

Or calls the gentle swell
Always towards yourself.
Always in one direction.

The rise
And fall again.

I've found my steady place.

I've built a safe harbour
Around your presence

And all my boats
Set sail from here.

Neap tides forever now.

GROWTH

So one day
The leaves
Turned
To the petals
And said -

We don't think
That all this
Worrying
Is getting us
Any Closer
To the sun,
You know.
And the petals,
Trembling slightly
In a faint breeze,
Replied -
We were never
Worrying
In the first place.

PRECIOUS THINGS

Some things
Are crystallised in time
Forever -
Like bugs caught
In amber.

Sunshine falling
Onto soft silky hair,
Catching a cheeky grin
Like a glint of crystal.

The sound of giggles
Filling a room
Like added decoration.

Hugs from small
Tender arms
Pressed in fine paper

Like a flower
In a book.

Tucked away
In my mind,
Like a gift.

To take out
And look at
Whenever
I want.

MY STORMY BOY

Lately, my boy
Walks in rainclouds.

He shoots lightning
At cheerful words

And challenges
Bring stormy tears.

I'd like to tell him
That I miss him.

But his face is wrapped
In thick mist like bandages.

The tender boy I knew -
Who curled chubby fingers in mine
And craved bedtime stories –
He won't emerge from this storm.

He is gone now.

And growing in his place,
This young man.

Obscured for now
By watery vapour.

I hope to meet him soon.

And though I may never see
His childish face again,
I know that small boy
Is holed up in there
In the gloom
With my growing man

Whispering in his ears
About rights and wrongs
And which best way to turn in a strong wind.

Like a compass
In his centre
Holding him straight.

PROUD MARY

Are you any good love?
Yeah, I'm ace!
Yeah? Well I'll be the judge of that....

I smile and dismiss him.
Get back to setting up.
He's obviously been on it all day,
And I hope he's not gonna be too much trouble.

This place is rife,
Like some sort of youth club
For overgrown kids
Still in their work clothes
After being let off early
Cos it's Friday.

But they get involved.
They're up dancing,
Enjoying the music
And not too rowdy.
My judge spends most
Of the night
Outside.
Smoking with his mates.

I'm halfway through my last set
When I see an old lady come in.
Stand at the bar by herself.
Incongruous here.
She's composed and classy.
And the little bit of my mind
That's not keeping an eye
On the over-enthusiastic dancers
In my face,

85

Wonders what brings her.

I'm just about on my last song
When the judge turns up –
Really out of it by now.
Do *Proud Mary*, do *Proud Mary!*
No chance mate – I just did it ten minutes ago!
He's not happy, gesturing and shouting
Something I can't hear
Above the music.

I carry on for half a song
And then he's back.
Do *Proud Mary*, do *Proud Mary!*
And now it's pissing me off.
You've got no chance.

He goes away and then just as I'm finishing
He's back.
This time on the stage
With his arm round my neck
Saying in my ear
Do *Proud Mary*, do *Proud Mary!*

He shouldn't be up here.
I can see people ready to pounce
But I don't think he means any harm.
Even if I don't wanna sing it again.

Look, I'm sorry but I only did it 20 minutes ago,
I can't do it again.

He looks at me, and then
Gestures to the old lady
Standing at the bar.
Yeah I know,

But me mam wa'n't in then.

And I realize that I've looked
And not seen
This lady - who's come out
On her own
At nearly 12 o clock,
To this place
On a Friday night,
To dance Tina Turner
With her son.

I wind my neck in,
Nod,
And do *Proud Mary*

Again.

THE TURN

Catching up with friends.
Glasses clinking, smoke rising –
A night in the pub.
When over the hubbub,
The sound of someone singing.
We look around
And see
The Turn.

Half-dismissed,
Half-forgotten,
Talk continues.
But I'm not listening now.
I'm watching,
Eyes glazed –

The same old thought
Drifting again
Through my mind.

I could do that.

I turn and tell
The people around the table
And they laugh.
You could as well.
Talk continues.

Fast forward a couple of years.
A different pub.
Different people.
Family gathers for some occasion
Or another.

The conversation
Turns toward
My new found singing career.

And there's a lull
In the noise
Around us.

I look up to see
The same glazed look I held
That other night.
But this time
In my Nanna's eyes.

She says
"I could have done that".
And with her eyes
Far away,

Looking back down the years,
She tells how she
Used to watch her mum
Singing in pubs.
Got up herself
The odd time.

But never
Had the nerve for it.

And I, shocked,
Glass in hand,
Take a moment
To count my blessings.

Thinking of all
Of those nerve-wracked nights
As shaking hands
Held the mic –
The bum notes,
The sarcastic comments,
The people not listening,
The fear of being
Too old
Or too crap.

How all of that
Was worth it
For this one moment.

DO YOUR WORK

When all the planning and dreaming is done
It's time to do your work.

When all the thinking and scheming is done
You have to do your work.

You've asked all your questions -
Now do your work.

You've got all your answers -
Now do your work.

The world's lying open -
Now do your work.

Do your work.
Do your work.
Do your work.

And when the sun is dying
And you're washed with pink and gold

When your heart is done with crying
When your stories are all told

When the flowers curl to closing
When the stars wake silver skies

When you've reaped your pages
Rich as corn and ache to close your eyes,

Rest easy on your pillow,
Rest easy in your sleep,
Be nourished by your fancy dreams

And breathe their colours deep.

For time will come a calling
And when it tips its hat
You'll know that you ate rich roast beef
When the calf was fat.

And you're leaving brimming storerooms
With riches to unfold.

Your heart is done with crying
And your stories are all told.

ON WHITBY PIER

On Whitby pier
Under darkening skies,
The waves declare war
On the beach,
The walls
And each other.

Mounting furious attacks
Before sliding away
To regroup,
Regain momentum.
Work up some speed
And run again
Pounding and racing.

We watch among
The passers by.
Amidst the squeals and shrieks
That rise to meet
Fireworks of foam and wet

As they fly in our faces and
Soak our feet.

I think that we're witness
To the power of air and sea today.
To its savagery and might.

But the Abbey,
Perched above us all
And clothed against
October weather,
In her full
Halloween glory,
Has seen it all before.

And I smile to think
How she's held strong
Against hundreds of years
Of days and hours and minutes
Of salty attacks,
Pelting elemental force
Against sturdy
Stone walls
That didn't give
Against them.

And the sea rages on
And the stones stand strong
And all is well
As we walk on.

WHY NOT HERE?

Where skin thins
Translucent
Like fallen autumn leaves.
Where tears and sweat
Flow like sap and rain
In sodden, muddy earth.
Where softness hardens
And melts.

Where we come
When it's time to go.

And if it must
Be somewhere,
Then why not here?

On clean sheets.
In bright glass rooms
Where we look out
Across field and forest
And remember how
We saw them
Through fresh spring budding,
Golden summer filters,
Bronze autumn fullness,
And white winter's truth.

Where beds are dressed
With friendly faces
And flashy outdoor colours.

If we must start
To say goodbye -
Then why not here?

In good company.
Where false fads and
Passing hurts
And old anger
Drop like loosened dying fruit
And are covered
By a softening drift
Of smiles and kind words -
Piling against and buffering
Pain and loss.

Where souls are loosened
Like wind in the trees
And set free to fly
Like birds.

Where naked branches
At last
Hide no secrets.

And standing stark
Against bright blank skies
We find that

Underneath the
Changing colours
Of our path
And long seasons

Etched there
In the bark

All along

Was love.

WHY I LOVE WHERE I LIVE

Because the pier
Where I sat alone
And whispered my pain
To the wind

Turns out to be
The same place
My parents
Walked together
Finding out love.

And also the place
Where my Nanna
Searched,
For a Father
She didn't know,
Amongst drinkers
In pubs
Where we
Still drink
Together now.

Because here,
My brother
And sisters
And me -
We breathe the same air.

And when we breathe out
The trees here
Breathe us in.

So that we are theirs
And they are ours,

And as their roots
Spread among the
Foundations
Of this city,
So ours stretch
And twine
Along alleys
Roads, pathways
And tenfoots.

Because the feet
That carried me
Before I carried
Myself
Walked the cobbles
And tarmac here.

And the feet that once
Pushed only up
Against my ribs
And down
Against my bladder,
Now find their way
Between the houses,
Spread out
From the heart
And spine
Of this place,
Of those who love them,
And make them laugh,
And teach them.

Because sometimes,
When my soul
Flies out of my mouth,

This is the place
That holds it,
Until I'm ready
To suck it
Back in.

Because the words
Of our lives
Have been printed
In its *Daily Mail*.
And the eyes
Of people here
Have taken in
Those abstract
Versions of minutes
We've lived.

So that we are theirs
And they are ours.

And when the next
Plague of words
Comes around
And all eyes rest
On these new
Broken moments,
Ours are wrapped
Around hot pattie and chips
And printed
Onto greasy batter
And eaten.

Because when people
Tell me that
This place
Smells of fish -

I'm surprised.

I never noticed.

And when people
Ask me
What do people from Hull
Call themselves?
I realise -
I've never thought of it.

And I'm confused.

Because I always thought
They knew us
By our vowels.
By the way we talk
With total strangers
And laugh at ourselves
And always say
We're sorry.

By the imprints
On the soles of our shoes
Of the fish trail.

Can't they see
We've wandered
Free museums
All our lives?
Looking upon whale bones,
Mammoths,
Viking ships
And freedom fighters?

That these things

Have made us cocky
And sure and proud
And unwilling
To name ourselves
For other people?

Because hands
That have
Laid rugby balls
On muddy try lines,
Thrown winning punches,
Stacked bricks,
Hauled trawler nets,
Coaxed valves and pipes,
Whisked eggs and flour
Into celebration meals -

Those are the hands

Of my people.

And this

Is my city.